Small Hotel

Rebecca Lenkiewicz's plays include *The Night Season* (National Theatre, Critics' Circle's Most Promising Playwright Award, 2004) and *Her Naked Skin* (National Theatre, 2008), which was the first play by a living female playwright to be staged on the Olivier stage. Other plays include *The Invisible* (The Bush), *Jane Wenham*, *Soho*, *The Painter* (Arcola), *The Typist* (Riverside Studios), *The Lioness* (Tricycle), *That Almost Unnameable Lust*, *Shoreditch Madonna*, *Blue Moon over Poplar* (Soho Theatre), *A Soldier's Tale* (Old Vic), *Invisible Mountains* (National Theatre), *Faeries* (Royal Opera House), *Justitia* (Peacock Theatre), and adaptations of Ibsen's *Ghosts* (Arcola), Strindberg's *Miss Julie* (Chichester Festival Theatre) and James's *The Turn of the Screw* (Almeida). Film includes *Colette*, *Disobedience* and *Ida*, co-written with Pawel Pawlikowksi, which won a BAFTA and the Oscar for Best Foreign Language Film, 2015. Most recent screenplays include *She Said*, *The Salt Path* and *Hot Milk*, which she also directed.

also by Rebecca Lenkiewicz from Faber

REBECCA LENKIEWICZ: PLAYS ONE
(*The Night Season, Shoreditch Madonna,
Her Naked Skin, The Painter*)

THE NIGHT SEASON
SHOREDITCH MADONNA
HER NAKED SKIN
THE PAINTER
JANE WENHAM, THE WITCH OF WALKERN
THE INVISIBLE

AN ENEMY OF THE PEOPLE
GHOSTS
(*after Ibsen*)

THE TURN OF THE SCREW
(*after Henry James*)

THE DANCE OF DEATH
(*after Strindberg*)

REBECCA LENKIEWICZ

Small Hotel

faber

First published in 2025
by Faber and Faber Limited
The Bindery, 51 Hatton Garden
London, EC1N 8HN

Typeset by Brighton Gray
Printed and bound in the UK by CPI Group (Ltd), Croydon CR0 4YY

All rights reserved
© Rebecca Lenkiewicz, 2025

Rebecca Lenkiewicz is hereby identified as author
of this work in accordance with Section 77 of the
Copyright, Designs and Patents Act 1988

All rights whatsoever in this work, amateur or professional,
are strictly reserved. Applications for permission for any use
whatsoever including performance rights must be made in
advance, prior to any such proposed use, to
Casarotto Ramsay & Associates Limited, 3rd Floor, 7 Savoy Court,
Strand, London WC2R 0EX (info@casarotto.co.uk)

No performance may be given unless a licence
has first been obtained

This book is sold subject to the condition that it shall not,
by way of trade or otherwise, be lent, resold, hired out
or otherwise circulated without the publisher's prior consent
in any form of binding or cover other than that in which
it is published and without a similar condition including
this condition being imposed on the subsequent purchaser

A CIP record for this book
is available from the British Library

ISBN 978–0–571–39919–2

Printed and bound in the UK on FSC® certified paper in line with our continuing
commitment to ethical business practices, sustainability and the environment.
For further information see faber.co.uk/environmental-policy

Our authorised representative in the EU for product safety is
Easy Access System Europe, Mustamäe tee 50, 10621 Tallinn, Estonia
gpsr.requests@easproject.com

2 4 6 8 10 9 7 5 3 1

Small Hotel was first performed at Theatre Royal Bath on 3 October 2025. The cast was as follows:

Larry / Richard Ralph Fiennes
Athena Francesca Annis
Marianne Rosalind Eleazar
Ava Rachel Tucker

Director Holly Race Roughan
Set Designer Bob Crowley
Costume Designer Loren Elstein
Lighting Designer Sally Ferguson
Composer & Sound Designer Max Pappenheim
Movement Director Sarah Fahie
Video Designer Luke Halls
Hair & Make-Up Designer Susanna Peretz
Casting Director Amy Ball CDG
Associate Director Emily Ling Williams

Acknowledgements

Rebecca Lenkiewicz would like to thank
Ralph Fiennes, Bob Crowley, Mel Kenyon, Danny Moar,
Dinah Wood, Dr Alan Cummings, Holly Race Roughan
and the brilliant Company.

Characters

Athena
seventies

Larry
sixty

Richard
sixty

Marianne
forty

Ava / Waitress / Receptionist / Singer
forties

Setting

The action takes place in various places.

Furniture should be minimal and fluid and a change of light or a projection should indicate a sense of place.

SMALL HOTEL

or

THE RECKONING

SCENE ONE

A Dream.
  In a red light Marianne stares at Larry.
  He taps a few steps with tap shoes; it's not a dance but more like thinking with his feet.
  Marianne takes off her coat, carefully, watching him. She thinks about taking off more but stops.

They stare at each other, silent.

Marianne taps with her tap shoes, expressing her thinking with the taps, not dancing.
  Larry starts to undress himself but stops when Marianne stops tapping.
  It's not sexy, it's about trust and suspicion and taking each other in . . .

A heartbeat sounds. Another heartbeat. They stop.

Marianne Put your clothes on, Larry.
  This isn't happening.

  Larry obeys and dresses himself. Marianne starts to walk away.

Larry Marianne.

  Reality.
    Larry and Marianne are in their own space. It's a phone call between them but no need for phones.

Voice (*American female*) I have Lorenz O'Dowd on the line for you.

Marianne That's fine . . .

  Marianne listens.

Larry Marianne . . . ?

Marianne . . . Hello Larry.

Larry Sorry . . .

He stops . . .

To . . . go through your agent. You got my email?

Marianne I did.

Larry But . . . you didn't respond . . .

Marianne No.

Larry Right . . . Shall I call you back on FaceTime would that be more . . . ?

Marianne This is fine.

Larry How are you?

Marianne I'm . . . here . . . You?

Larry I'm . . . good. Yes . . . I'm alive . . . Sorry if this is a surprise.

Marianne I like surprises. How are you?

Larry I'm okay. Working . . . busy . . . married.

Marianne Do people still do that?

Larry They do. I did. Twice. I've been married twice.

Marianne And this one is good?

Larry Yes it's . . . good.

Marianne You don't sound very sure?

Larry The first was so bad. It's hard to compare.

Marianne laughs.

But you . . . You've done brilliantly. I've watched all your films.

Marianne Not the mermaid. Please not that.

Larry I enjoyed the mermaid.

Marianne Then you're still crazy. Although actually the fish were beautiful . . .

They take a moment.

It's been twenty years, Larry.

Larry I know. How are you?

Marianne I've been thinking about forgiveness a lot. So why do you want me on your show?

Larry Everyone wants an interview with you.

Marianne I'm not good at all of that.

Larry I'm sure you're brilliant.

Marianne I'm not. I don't do it. But you had that huge late night show? And now this one is . . . what?

Larry It's smaller. A different channel.

Marianne What happened to the old show?

Larry It . . . deteriorated.

Marianne . . . And do you have children?

Larry I don't. You don't?

Marianne (*with an American accent*) 'Copy that.'

Larry I realise this is . . . strange. And obviously I'd just love to see you and to talk.

Marianne It's not obvious. You haven't contacted me in two decades.

Larry It would be a big boost. For the show. We'd get you here and put you up somewhere nice.

Marianne Does it need a boost?

Larry More of a rocket . . . We're possibly going under. Your being on it would be a complete coup. Pure adrenaline.

Marianne I really am bad in interviews though Larry and I'll tell you why . . .

Larry Are you happy?

Marianne I'm . . . the happiest I've been . . . Yeah.

Larry Good . . . And home is LA.

Marianne San Francisco now. I have a big garden.

Larry Good. That sounds nice.

Marianne I go to a lot of meetings. AA meetings.

Larry Okay . . . We both should have probably gone to AA in New York instead of clubbing.

Marianne Your booze was recreational. I've been drinking since I was nine.

Larry I was . . . booted off the big evening show because I was pissed. Nobody watching would know but you know . . .

Marianne And did you stop drinking?

Larry I cut down. It's not a problem. I couldn't really do what I do without it. The social part.

Marianne I'll think about the show, Larry.

Larry If you were to do it we could and should meet beforehand. Don't you think?

Marianne That's alright. I know what you look like.

Larry Have you seen the show?

Marianne I saw the other one when you talked to Anjelica Huston.

Larry Ah yes. She was great.

Marianne And then I saw you selling suitcases on a shopping channel.

Larry That was in the interim . . . They were executive briefcases . . . No matter.

Marianne Do you still support your brother and your mother?

Larry I do. Yes.

Marianne takes this in, admires Larry's loyalty.

Marianne Your eyes looked different. When you were doing those adverts.

Larry It wasn't an advert . . . it was a . . . campaign . . .

Larry laughs at himself.

. . . How are you?

Marianne That's the third time you've asked me that.

Larry I'm a better interviewer on telly. I'm a bit . . .

Marianne I know . . . I've thought about you.

Larry With warmth?

Marianne With warmth.

Larry It's very nice . . . to hear your voice.

Marianne We had an intense time.

Larry Insane in many ways . . . shall I wait for your people to let me know then?

Marianne I'll text you. It wasn't insane.

Larry I meant that I was.

Marianne Okay. Later.

Larry Your voice hasn't changed. Those plays you did in those tiny places.

Marianne It has changed. Larry, I'd probably . . . overshare in an interview.

Larry That's not a problem. That would make our producers ecstatic. They haven't got a creative thought between all of them . . . Do you still smoke?

Marianne Why?

Larry I just . . . want to know.

Marianne I would be honest in an interview. I can't not be.

Larry I'd expect nothing less. And so would I. It's sort of my . . . trademark.

Marianne takes this strange sentence in.

Marianne They have you. They have a hold of you . . . I forgive you Larry.

And Marianne hangs up.

A Dream.
 The sound of the landline going dead morphs into a life support machine which morphs into lift music.

A desolate bar. Liverpool.
 Larry, dishevelled, sits with a rep, Ava, forties, female. She wears an eyepatch.

Ava So you know where you are?

Larry Yes. Yes I'm in this bar . . . and . . . we're in . . . ?

Ava Liverpool . . . But you don't know how you got here?

Larry . . . I was at a train station? And I'm . . . meeting people? Women.

Ava Five women. But you're early, Lorenz. Do you know where you're staying tonight?

Larry A hotel. There's a small hotel.

Ava Tonight would be quite . . . intense . . . It's meant to be . . . fun . . . you know?

Larry It's speed . . . something about speed.

Ava Speed dating. Maybe you should get some air? Have a walk around the docks?

Larry I haven't stopped walking . . . for days . . . Please . . . let me sit down and stop walking . . . Your . . . eye.

Ava Is my eye.

Larry Can I get a double vodka?

Ava takes Larry's wallet from his pocket. She takes money out.

Ava I'll set up a tab.

Ava does not move. Instead she looks through Larry's wallet, his various and many cards, skimming them away from her as she reads each one.

Rewards. Rewards. Rewards.

'There's a Small Hotel' sung by Jack Whiting (1937) starts to play while Ava frisks Larry, emptying his pockets of their contents. He laughs as she tickles him.

This is serious, Larry. It's security. Knives in your boot or blades in your heel.

Larry I know I know.

But he just keeps laughing with what feels like tickling. Ava finds bubblegum and blows bubbles with it. As the song plays, Larry starts to move slowly to it . . . trying to remember events. He checks his body slowly . . . his wrists, his fingers . . . for bruises or cuts.

I like this song. It's unexpected. I was born here.

Ava goes to a microphone and sings the third verse of 'There's a Small Hotel'...

The grim place turns into a palace of light with shimmering lights.

Larry sees his mother Athena who walks onto the dance floor. He goes to her.

Ava hums quietly.

Athena Larry... My Larry... what are you doing here?

Larry I don't know, Mother.

Athena But you knew I came here... When I was sixteen... I smuggled you and Richard onto the boat. Both of you in one tiny pram. And I was so sick, Larry. The sea was so rough... But I got away from them. I brought you away from that horrific place. And then to London. We fed the pigeons.

Larry and Athena dance together, while Ava sings the next few lines.

Ava hums.

But why are you here? Where's your brother?

Larry He's living on a farm.

Athena I know that but what is he doing? I wish you would both decide about things... You must have come here because I did. You wanted to see where you came from? As a boy... You would never leave me alone. You were always bringing me things...

Larry Mother...

Athena Drawings... or dead animals...

Athena laughs, soft, warm. Larry holds Athena and they dance beautifully together.

Ava sings the next few lines of the song.

I have to go, Larry. I need to check out . . . I'm late. But you . . . you shouldn't be here. It's too early for you. Larry? You must stay!

Larry Mother . . . Athena . . .

Athena goes back into the shadows. It's dark and quiet.

The light is very bright . . .

It's not.

And there's this . . . ringing in my ears . . .

Ava I know you. Are you a politician?

Larry laughs. Ava laughs.

Larry I was meant to go home to my wife.
But she's left me. And then I was following Marianne.

Ava And you thought speed dating was a good idea? Meeting five women? For five minutes each?

Larry Five good minutes might be the most I can give to someone.

Ava What do you want from tonight, Lorenz?
. . . Oblivion? Comfort? Sex? You won't get any of that. You won't go home with any of these women. One of them will want a relationship. Another will want a child. One will be depressed. And one will be too nice. Do you see?

Larry What about the last one? You said five?

Ava There'll be no skin on skin. You won't score.

Larry Maybe I don't want that . . . Maybe I'm not craving . . . physicality. I might need a cigarette . . . Why wouldn't I score?

Ava Go home, Larry . . . You're just the sort of mess that some women fall for. Hope is fucking precious you know. So go.

Larry What happened to your eye?

Ava Acid. From the boy next door. I told him I was seeing someone else. I wasn't.
You're haunted by someone.

Larry Your scar . . . can I see it?

Ava hesitates . . . then takes off her eyepatch and Larry looks at her scar which is in fact a normal eye. He glances at her name badge too. Ava puts her patch back on.

I think you're wonderful . . . Ava. Brave and brilliant.

Ava So shall I cross you off this list?

Larry Perhaps that's a good idea, Ava. Perhaps you're right.

Larry touches his face.

Do my eyes really look different?

Ava I don't know how you normally look, Lorenz.

Ava straightens him out a bit. She adjusts his jacket and sees that his shirt is bloodied around his heart and stomach.

That's blood? Lorenz, it's blood. You need a . . . towel . . . or a vet.

Larry It's not mine . . . it's not my blood! I didn't take it! It wasn't me . . .

Ava wants to leave . . .
  Larry holds her wrists, not threatening but intent.

There's something blunt . . . lodged . . . inside me . . . Like when I climbed the trees with Richard. When we were boys. And he hit me with that branch. Can you see me, Ava? Can you?

Ava and Larry stare at each other. She half understands.

They stand up and do a quick tap dance just staring at each other...

When you come out of the trees and the leaves at the top it's so bright. I refuse. I refuse to leave her!

Larry taps and walks into the next scene, determined to see Marianne.

SCENE TWO

Reality.
  A few days before.
  A make-up room in a TV studio.
  A make-up artist helps Larry to look pristine.

Larry phones his twin, Richard, who appears on a screen.
  They are identical but Richard has a beard and is generally scruffy-looking, unkempt, where Larry is impeccably casually smart.
  They have very different energies.
  Larry is unusually nervous about his upcoming interview but contains it.

Richard Lorenz.

Larry Why are you calling me Lorenz?

Richard I thought I might try it while you're at work. Like the others do.

Larry You okay? I haven't got long.

Richard I'm good to go, no need to linger... Speak tomorrow then?

Larry Well I've got six minutes.

Richard Ah, six is a lot... Who are you talking to tonight?

Larry Marianne Barre. You met her.

Richard Marianne? Your Marianne?

Larry Not so much mine now. That was a couple of decades ago.

Richard Yes and she wasn't yours then really. Didn't I ply her with wild flowers? I called her my queen?

Larry Yes. When I brought her home to meet Mother.

Richard And what did Mother make of her?

Larry Mother wasn't home. She was in Denmark Hill.

Richard That's right. But Mother was still terrified she'd steal you off. Back to New York.

Larry She was. She screamed at me in front of all the staff and visitors. Really screamed.

Richard I never went there did I? I got as far as the train station once and then I came straight back . . . Marianne is a queen . . . You were together a long time. Well you might get a real audience tonight.

Larry Yeah . . . Have you been busy?

Richard I've been composting. And I needed to sand some of the plastering. I'm always busy. Various stuff. Sorting . . . Are you going to talk to any scientists soon?

Larry Not that I know of. Do you ever get a slight ticking . . . or . . . clicking . . . in your ear? As if there was something inside it?

Richard What, like a cockroach?

Larry I'm hoping not a cockroach . . .

Richard Is it connected to your knee pain? Have you been frying the turmeric with the black pepper? And drinking the olive oil?

Larry I've no time to do that, Richard. And the knee's not a problem . . . it just hurts to sit still.

Richard Does she live in Los Angeles now? Can you ask her about the water system in California? About the high levels of arsenic and chromium in drinking water? And the storm water pollution in the ocean?

Larry We'll be talking film.

Richard I don't mean actual statistics just awareness . . . Are people aware of the situation? Is anyone talking about it . . . if you could ask her about that it would be really useful . . . to air it . . . nationally.

Larry Marianne never does TV interviews. She's like a modern-day Garbo.

Richard Please talk to her . . . about the water . . . just for a minute . . .

Larry There'll be no time for that.

Richard Why don't you suggest extending it so that you can talk about the pollution issues?

Larry We're live. In half an hour. And then the news is straight after us.

Richard Ask her, Larry? It's important . . . it's far more important than *Celebrity Shagz*.

Larry I'm not talking to her about celebrity shags. Fuck's sake.

Richard Sorry. That just came out. I didn't call it that.

Larry What are you talking about?

Richard It doesn't matter.

Larry Who calls it that?

Richard Mother. It's her name for your show. *Celebrity Shagz*. With a Z.

Larry It's an in-depth talk. And sometimes I ask braver questions than other interviewers.

Richard It's not me. It's Athena. You know she loves to . . . rename everything.

Larry sighs . . . this isn't helping him.

You're a bit . . . you seem a bit . . . are you? It was a really nice sky around here tonight. I stopped taking my pills and it's really helping.

Larry Good. I need to get on now.

Richard Okay. Bye Larry.

Larry In a minute . . .

Richard What else then? Don't you need to get your make-up done?

Larry It's done. Is it okay?

Richard Oh . . . come closer.

Larry holds the phone closer to himself.

Subtle. They're very clever.

Larry Clever how? What's wrong with it?

Richard Nothing. Show me again.

Richard just looks at it, puzzled . . .

It's fine. You don't want to look like Dirk Bogarde in *Death in Venice* . . . The pylons seemed very loud today. I talked to Mother today . . .

Larry Can we stop about Athena . . . I need some energy.

Richard She wants to see that film. I can't take her. Obviously.

Larry She'll hate it.

Richard Anyway she's got this theory about us . . . she's going to share it with me tomorrow.

Larry Okay. Well, speak tomorrow?

Richard Yeah . . . seven or eight thirty tomorrow? Wait . . . I've written something on my hand.

Richard reads his own scrawl.

It's these pills. They affect my short term memory. Okay yes. Mother said can you book her into an eight o'clock screening tonight. And book her a cab.

Larry Fine. I'll do it now. Is my make-up okay?

Richard It's fantastic. Camouflage. Bye Larry. Have a good night. Say hello to Marianne from me. Tell her that I've watched her films. I liked the one with the otters. She must love wildlife . . . it wasn't a great part. And the one where she smashed up that room. I'll report back on Athena's theory. It's new she said, and startling.

Larry Great. Okay . . . I'd better go.

Richard It's going to be a good sunset actually. Bye Larry. I'll watch the show.

Larry Thanks Richard.

Richard That chef last week was a bit boring wasn't he? He didn't seem to want to talk about cooking. Just . . . cars.

Larry Yeah. See you.

Richard hangs up. Larry sighs, he starts to book a film ticket, feeling guilty about Richard.
He rings Athena who sits in a chair in her flat.

Mother it's Larry.

Athena Larry. Lovely. Are you coming round?

Larry I've got the show. This film you want to see. You know it's a sort of body horror?

Athena Don't infantilise me Larry. Just book the eight o'clock. And I need a taxi there and back.

Larry It's just quite . . . graphic.

Athena I've had two children. One of them was you.

Larry Fine. I just know you don't like . . . fluids.

Athena I've had two babies hurtle out of me. In seconds. Blood. Everything imaginable.

Larry Fine. I'll ring you tomorrow?

Athena I've something important to talk to you about. Not on the phone. And I need Brasso and the usual stuff.

Larry I'll come round then. In the afternoon. Enjoy your night.

Athena You just said I wouldn't.

Larry Bye Athena.

Athena Goodbye Richard. Thank you.

Larry Larry.

Athena Yes. Goodbye Larry. My Larry.

Larry hangs up, breathes and inspects his make-up and does some mouth stretches and voice exercises to warm up.

SCENE THREE

Reality.
A TV studio.
Larry sits opposite Marianne Barre. She is warm and the audience are enjoying their rapport. They have been talking a while.
Larry is very much 'on' and completely charming and Marianne is warm and responsive.

Larry I can't believe that you've only given one in-depth interview before . . . throughout your entire film career?

Marianne They can't force you?

Larry I felt it would come with the territory.

Marianne The one I did, it wasn't a good experience . . . did you see it?

Larry I thought it was wonderful. Honest and fascinating.

Marianne That was the end result. There was a lot of editing. That was necessary.

Larry Okay . . . well we're live so . . . no scissors here . . .

They both laugh . . .

Marianne Exactly . . . we're walking on that tightrope between the Twin Towers . . .

Larry But you must . . . enjoy privacy?

Marianne The work is the work . . . and my life, my opinions . . . they're . . . something separate. So I'll happily talk about a movie for a sound bite or to give it a push . . . but . . .

Marianne stops . . .

Larry Understood . . . and you've stopped making films for a while? Is that the case?

Marianne Directors can be vampires you know . . . not all. But when it happens you need a while . . . to . . .

Larry To . . . recalibrate?

Marianne Recalibrate. Recover. To reclaim yourself actually. You've been emotionally hijacked . . . and . . . you need to return. Unharmed.

Larry I'm sorry . . . that it can be that intense.

Marianne It can be painful . . . It's . . . power. Hierarchies. There's no place for that in an artistic workspace. No need. And it inhibits.

Larry What are the conditions then, that you crave? To make something.

Marianne Space. Trust. Interesting people. Just . . . ideas . . . A good room.

Larry And on a film set you need someone to lead but not to dictate?

Marianne In some moments or scenes even leading can be too strong. Holding maybe . . .

Larry And how do you handle it? When something feels toxic?

Marianne You just have to . . . navigate . . . and it's tiring . . . you first meet a director and it's cakes and tea and more cakes more cakes . . . and then they try to . . . manipulate you . . . They trespass. They become trespassers. And then a dictatorship . . . it was great when people used to smoke on these shows wasn't it? Bette Davis . . . she was an amazing actor . . . a chameleon . . .

Larry nods, smiles, is fascinated at seeing Marianne again.

Larry The range of parts you play is quite incredible.

Marianne It would be dull to simply repeat . . .

Larry And you inhabit them with such honesty. Would you describe yourself as a 'method' actor?

Marianne (*indicates no*) I sort of become my role for a while . . . I have a different process . . .

Larry Can you share it with us?

Marianne It's . . . private.

Larry But you'd share it with a director? On set?

Marianne Would I?

They laugh . . .

Larry Whatever you do it works. You've won an Oscar. And two Baftas. And this process . . . ?

Marianne . . . It's about rhythm.

Larry In the words?

Marianne In everything. The thought, the breathing. Everything. It's also about trust.

Larry Is it difficult, knowing who to trust?

Marianne You Larry . . . You're asking me that?

Marianne laughs . . . then thinks about the question. Larry clocks their history for a moment.

Larry Don't . . . answer if . . . if you don't want to . . .

Marianne It's not about what I want . . . it needs to be addressed . . .

Larry waits as Marianne thinks. She is warm and enthused but Larry is slightly worried . . .

Larry We can park that . . . come back to it?

Marianne No no . . . I'm thinking . . .

Marianne places herself back at various times, to piece it all together; she is slightly away and Larry watches her, rapt.

What was the actual question again?

Larry No matter . . . You voiced an animation last year . . . I enjoyed watching that mermaid.

Marianne But the other question was more interesting?

Larry How or who did you trust?

Marianne . . . it was 'Is it difficult to know who to trust?'

Larry Yes. But . . .

Marianne But do you mean in life? Or work?

Larry In either. Or both.

Larry really looks at her, the woman he has thought of often for almost two decades, Marianne looks at him and knows it is important.

Marianne Fuck . . . I knew it would be strange seeing you after this long a time. But I didn't realise . . . I can't quite . . . think straight . . .

Larry It's great to see you too.

Marianne Is there a buzzing in here? Like . . .

Marianne indicates her ear. They both listen . . . there's no external buzzing. Larry indicates his ear . . .

Larry I hear it, yes.

And they both listen for moments to a buzzing in their own ears but it's not external. Marianne gets out some cigarettes. Larry watches . . .

Marianne You want one?

She smiles, it's complicit. She takes out two cigarettes and puts them in her mouth, then gives an unlit cigarette to

Larry. They both look at each other, then eat their candy cigarettes. It's their old joke. Marianne laughs, open, warm.

How come you married twice? You said you'd never marry.

Larry Did I say that? I was younger.

Marianne Thirty-nine . . . But how is it? Did you ever do that couples' therapy thing ?

Larry takes a moment . . . embraces the public 'honesty'.

Larry We did. Yes we have.

Marianne There's an industry isn't there? Built out of welding unhappy people to their marital bed . . .

Larry I imagine most couples appreciate the help? Professional help.

Marianne But if it's really 'love' does it need help? Maybe it's just gone. Why is promiscuous seen as . . . wrong . . . and a long term relationship as somehow right . . . unless the promiscuity is dishonest. That's yeah . . .

Larry deflects.

Larry Are you in a relationship? Does work allow for that?

Marianne I do what I want. And you . . . Maybe it's better to just . . . move on if you're chronically bored. Are you?

Larry drinks some water, he is wrong-footed.
Larry's knees hurt with the sitting still and he tries to hide it. He stands up for a moment and pretends it hasn't happened.

Are you okay?

Larry Perfect . . . We touched on awards. Process. Money . . .

Marianne We did, Larry . . . we touched . . .

They look at each other. They touched a lot in a past life. Larry reins them back in.

Larry So *Wisconsin Nights* was your breakout role . . . in the raging scene . . . how much of that was scripted?

Marianne It's all improvised . . . but if you really want to talk about LA, Larry . . . talk about the water . . . Not Hollywood. Talk about arsenic, talk about chromium in the drinking water. Use your platform. Really use this. And the water corporations. Who get away with it and get rich every time. And the storm pollution in the bays? If it rains or storms then the drains overflow and it's terrifying . . . Are you interested?

Larry Yes.

Marianne Are you though? How is the Thames? And your rural rivers?

Larry They're . . . flowing. 'Old Mother Thames' and the rest . . .

Marianne nods, knows he's not interested.

Marianne (*in an American accent*) Copy that.

Larry waits a moment, then dives back in.

Larry We met in New York when you were first auditioning. You were very brilliant in that Edward Albee play.

Marianne I was. *The American Dream.* I've no idea why. I was sleeping on people's sofas . . . And New York was different? . . . I had nothing . . . but I was . . . intensely happy. There was the grandmother who kept shouting 'The boxes the boxes!' . . . I didn't know what it meant then . . . but I do now . . .

Larry And you just played Blanche DuBois on Broadway. Did you love her?

Marianne I did . . . It's Blanche against the world. And she was such an incredible champion for women, you know? Kowalski represents everyone who has ever laid a controlling or violent finger on every female . . . And she's only thirty years old in the play . . . thirty . . . And he describes her as an aging Southern beauty . . .

Larry Natasha in *War and Peace* worries about being old. And she's nineteen.

Marianne But Mitch he's even worse. At least Stanley is an honest thug. Mitch controls and projects . . . And Blanche she fights so hard . . . but . . .

Larry And you received a Tony.

Marianne Yeah but I was just saying something then Larry . . .

Larry Please . . .

Marianne It doesn't matter. Just . . . the gift of Williams's poetry . . .

Marianne switches off slightly due to the interruption of her thoughts . . .

What else? Do people vape? I have a vape.

Larry There'll be alarms . . . we'll have to leave the building . . . unless you have an edible vape?

Marianne We'd have to go down a fire escape? . . . Best not to then . . . And what else?

Larry can sense Marianne isn't playing the game any more and tries to steer her back.

Larry You seem to baulk against Hollywood but you stayed there? You didn't want to move back to New York or abroad?

Marianne I get confused sometimes . . . with timelines . . . and places . . . I wish you had let me talk more freely about Blanche.

Larry Let's . . . rewind . . . How did you . . . feel? When they cast you as Blanche DuBois?

Marianne Why shouldn't I play Blanche? I'm a woman.

And Marianne sort of stops . . . and the energy stops. Larry waits. Marianne drinks some water, seems deflated . . .

Larry Are you okay?

The actor playing Marianne stops acting, as does Larry. In this instance they are Rosalind and Ralph.

Ralph Are you okay, Ros?

Rosalind Me? Are you asking me, Ralph?

Rosalind is herself as is Ralph . . .

They look at each other and take each other in . . . until they are ready to go back into the words..
  Rosalind speaks a haiku. The actors are still themselves.

love's many forms –
all the threads of desire
begin in purest white

Ralph
over my shoulder
I saw her under her umbrella
just a glance

Rosalind You did.

Ralph Shall we?

Rosalind Dance? Dance for them 'Larry'? Sure?

And 'Larry' and 'Marianne' get back into character and on script by dancing a quick show tap dance for the audience, then try to locate the moment they left from . . .

Larry Are you okay?

I'm sorry if I rushed you . . .

Marianne I have very specific memories of you, Larry. Of you and me.

Larry . . . Shall we talk about your Broadway career?

Marianne Tony Tony Tony.

Marianne laughs.

I liked our time in New York. You found yourself doing a play one minute and when it ended you might be intimate with someone on a street corner.

Larry nods. Processes this.

Mightn't you?

Larry Yes.

Marianne You remember that? In the dark? All the lights everywhere but we were under that fire escape. And a cat was watching us?

Larry waits . . .

Larry Yes. I remember. Cut back to the *Wisconsin Nights* scene. What did you think of to enrage you while you trashed the room?

Marianne I'd just look around me . . . Or if I wanted rage on a personal level . . . I thought of you.

Larry nods, cautious.

Larry We need to wrap it up soon Marianne but thank you for being so incredible.

Marianne I'm not incredible but I can act because I feel it so deeply, Larry . . . and I remember details . . . I remember why you were called Larry even. And your brother is Richard. Because of the songwriters. Rodgers and Hart. Your mother loved them. Who did you marry?

Larry Lynne. And then Theresa. Now I'm married to Theresa.

Marianne Your eyes really are different. But you're happy?

Larry Happy . . . I was happy . . . taking the subway to Brighton Beach with you and watching you swim in the rain . . . and just loving looking at people . . . their faces . . . and eating hunks of cholla bread on the grey sand . . . and then . . . and then . . .

Marianne And then becomes now.

Larry . . . I'm still capable of joy . . . but those moments aren't connected to what my daily life is . . . they're separate . . . I do experience . . . euphoria . . . just seeing the sky . . . or watching a dog run along a beach . . . or swimming in a cold river . . . or looking at a tree . . . so that . . . capacity . . . is still there . . . I've probably said too much . . .

Marianne You haven't said enough.

Marianne really looks at him and he looks at her. Marianne goes in to kiss Larry and he kisses her back. They kiss and kiss.

Larry . . .

Larry Yes.

Marianne I was so young Larry.

Larry We were all young.

Marianne You not so much. I was nineteen. You were thirty-nine.

Larry is suddenly aware of the public situation.

Larry . . . I don't even think of an age gap when I think of . . . that time.

Marianne You must remember. We first fucked on your fortieth birthday. That was my present to you.

Larry is getting messages through his earpiece to wrap up and he's stressed but tries to smooth it.

Larry . . . I just remember you as being funny. And mature . . . emotionally.

Marianne Because I had to be . . . You knew what I'd been through. I'd used sex as a means of warmth and gaining attention since I was fourteen. You knew that. And you knew why I was like that. What had happened to me the years before that.

Larry Our . . . brief . . . relationship was . . . consensual. And . . . good . . . wasn't it?

Marianne Is a year brief?

Larry I don't think we're attaching blame here . . . I'm just stating facts.

Marianne I'm not talking about criminal either. I'm talking about opportunistic. I'm talking about control. I'm talking about letting teenagers fuck teenagers, not middle-aged men.

Larry . . . We have to stop it there. But thank you Marianne. You really are . . . incredible. Thank you.

Marianne walks out. Larry sits, disrupted, disturbed.

SCENE FOUR

Reality.
Larry sorts boxes of books while on a WhatsApp video call to Richard.

Larry Fuck . . . fuck . . . fuck.

Richard Larry I'm telling you. Again. A lot of people get cancelled now. Everywhere. Everywhere Larry. It's rife. It's not a problem.

Larry And I told you. I'm not cancelled. I can't really talk Richard. They're having a meeting about me now and then Balfour is calling me with a debrief in maybe . . . ten minutes. It could be sooner if they decide quickly.

Richard Right, understood . . . but you only have to look at a paper. Or . . . everyone. Priests. Teachers. Writers. Politicians, well that's a given.

Larry I haven't been cancelled.

Richard Everything that's toxic, everything gets picked up. You can't have placards in plays any more.

Larry I'm not cancelled. I'm on a leave of absence. I might be back to work next week.

Richard You think? Possibly . . . There are much worse cases than yours. Awful things. Yours will blow over, no one's that interested. And there are new things like body shaming.

Larry I kissed Marianne. That's all I did.

Richard And the age thing. It's not criminal as you said but people love a slogan.

Larry You're not helping here.

Larry Sorry . . . And Theresa?

Larry Has given me a day to pack and get out.

Richard What did she say?

Larry It was like a speech . . . it was very clear and detailed, you know . . . absolute rage but she was sort of enjoying it in some way I think.

Richard Did she cite a list of wrongdoing?

Larry A long list.

Richard I knew she'd make a list. I've never liked Theresa. At least with Lynne she adored you and you knew there was some damage there somewhere . . . It's different with Theresa . . . I don't think she's ever liked you that much, Larry. I think in some ways she really can't stand you.

Larry But you didn't think to say that in the last seven years?

Richard It's not really useful information is it? Athena was raging.

Larry About my being suspended?

Richard That, yes. But also you forgot to book her a taxi back. I had to do it. I'd deleted the app but I resuscitated it. I used to love Ubering. Anyway I managed it. I got her a cab home. And she found the film pretty challenging, it made her feel sick.

Larry . . . I was backstage with Balfour shouting at me.

Richard I told her that. I didn't think Balfour was capable of rage. He always looks so . . . flat.

Larry What does Athena think? About all of this?

Richard She laughed a lot . . . about how Theresa would react . . . Is Theresa going to keep the car? What about my lifts?

Larry You'll have to get an Uber. You've got the app now. Or a bus.

Richard And Athena's theory – did you listen to my message?

Larry No. I didn't see a message. It's this phone.

Richard What she said was really sad and repellent . . . she'll tell you herself . . . Are you going to see Marianne again?

Larry I don't know.

Richard And the house is Theresa's. You can leave with just a bag . . . Do you remember our father turning up with just a holdall . . . when we were seven . . . and we didn't even know him?

Larry I thought he'd come to fix something. I've got to take this call with Balfour soon.

Richard Don't talk to him, Larry, he's meant to be loyal. You show them something real and live and they all run away . . .

Larry It'll blow over. What was this repellent thing Athena said?

Richard I can't say it all again. The message definitely sent. I checked it. The recording was eleven minutes long. And I've pinged you some useful links on WhatsApp. About other people being cancelled. Yes and I told you to come and live with me.

Larry What?

Richard Here. There's an upstairs bit. A sort of mezzanine. And I'd build an extra wall so I don't get a chemical headache from you.

Larry A mezzanine? In your barn? I've never seen that.

Richard Because you never look up . . . You have to look up more, Larry . . . have a look at trees and cloud formations . . . they really help . . . Turner used to do it a lot. He would just walk or sit looking up and waiting for the right cloud formation. And then paint it.

Larry I still can't picture this mezzanine . . . show it to me . . .

Richard turns his phone camera to the upper part of the barn. All hay and debris.

You just mean where all the hay is.

Richard I'd move the hay. I don't mean forever. I don't think I could live with you permanently. But for a while. A year or two.

Larry I'm okay thanks, Dick. And you'd have a chemical reaction even if there was a wall, wouldn't you?

Richard But this is an emergency . . . Why did you call me Dick?

Larry Sorry.

Richard You're feeling cruel. Understood. But that would dissipate here. The views are wonderful. Good trees. Old trees. And they really give you just such . . . brilliant advice . . . and ballast . . . Trees look after each other you know . . .

Larry They're better than fucking humans then aren't they?

Richard You're depressed. It's chemical right now but it will allay. You just need volition . . . and certainty . . . And look this will cheer you up . . . that Zoom meditation gift token that you bought for me . . . that was almost expired . . . that you said was going to be a waste . . . yes? I used it . . . last night. Three hours before the year was up? Seems like ten years ago you sent it to me. Anyway it was really good. Really helpful.

Larry I'm glad. That's really good. Listen Richard . . . Balfour's going to call me in a minute. I just need to. prepare a bit.

Richard Everyone was old on it. Older than us even. Except for Katarina. Who was actually really nice. We got caught in the kind of aftermath goodbye bit. We were the only two boxes left. I couldn't see how to leave the meeting and then I didn't actually want to because she kept talking to me and laughing. She looks like Anna Magnani. She's Romanian. She lives in Bradford. I read her a bit of Walt Whitman.

Larry That's really nice, Richard.

Richard She's a forty-year-old widow. Her husband was a drunk and was killed by a tank when he was coming back from a pub one night . . . it was just a random tank, it wasn't in a war.

Larry Right . . . Shit.

Richard I don't think she was that upset actually. She didn't dwell on it . . . She lives alone . . . she's religious. She's very funny. I laughed a bit too loud . . . and I read her some Walt Whitman.

Larry ignores Richard's repeat.

Larry Yes? That's great.

Richard It was just nice to . . . communicate. We talked about all sorts . . . Don't mention it to mother.

Larry Course not. Why would I do that?

Richard Exactly. But we talked about her water bill. Her new smart water meter. I explained how they actually work. You see if you'd talked about the water with Marianne . . . if you'd known the chromium content you could have discussed that . . . and you wouldn't have been cancelled.

Richard laughs. Larry laughs.

Also if you're downsizing or getting rid of stuff? If you're leaving? Can I have your binoculars and your tent? I'll bleach them so they're safe. How much mould is there in your house right now would you say? And your Ordnance Survey maps. Or you might need them actually . . . and they might be a bit toxic. But maybe Dad's pipe.

Larry I don't want the fucker's pipe. I don't know even know why it's here. Or how I got it.

Richard What Athena said . . .

Richard goes quiet . . . is troubled.

Larry It can't have been that bad, Richard? I mean she's said the worst stuff a mother can say?

Richard This was different . . . I don't want it either. I don't want his fucking pipe. Or your stuff. I don't want any of it.

Richard twitches a bit; he seems on the verge of being really upset.

Larry What? What did she say, Richard?

Richard breathes a bit deeper, trying not to be upset as Larry talks.

Richard? What? Tell me?

Richard I've just had enough you know . . . of being ill and . . . It's difficult when you go backwards and . . . our relationship . . . you, my brother . . . it means you know . . . a lot to me . . .

Richard tries not to cry.

Anyway . . . If I were you . . . I'm not . . . but if I were . . . I would contact Marianne . . . So it's not all for nothing . . . Nothing should be for nothing . . .

And Richard suddenly breaks down.

Larry Richard?

Richard can't respond.

Richard . . . Richard . . . whatever she said she was probably drunk . . .

Richard speaks through tears.

Richard She was, she was. But it's not just that . . . Do your call . . . just do your call . . .

Larry The call doesn't matter . . .

Richard It does. It does. Go.

Richard hangs up. Larry is both troubled and relieved, guilty. He almost rings Richard back but doesn't. Larry waits. The phone rings.

Larry Balfour? How are you?

Balfour (*voice-over*) Lorenz . . . I'm okay thanks. You?

Larry Yeah . . . how did the meeting go? What did they say?

Balfour (*voice-over*) It didn't happen. Sorry, mate. Alan suddenly couldn't make it. And Stephanie wants to be present. And tomorrow I'm working from home. So we're aiming for early next week.

Larry takes this in, Balfour's not letting him know sooner. Contains his emotion and rage.

Larry . . . Right . . . Just I've been . . . So no one's feeling a . . . sense of urgency?

Balfour (*voice-over*) It is priority. It's just people's schedules.

Larry Do you have any sense of how it will go?

Balfour (*voice-over*) I can't really say, Lorenz, not now. Sorry, mate. I've got to go . . .

Larry But am I technically . . . employed at the moment or not?

Balfour (*voice-over*) That might be more HR than me. But it's all too early to say. But I don't like doing these group calls at home. With kids around.

Larry What does that mean?

Balfour (*voice-over*) Nothing, I just mean logistics. You understand?

Larry Right. Bye.

Larry presses a button on his phone, crouches, puts his phone in his pocket and sort of holds himself.

Sorry you can't talk right now, Balfour. Sorry, mate . . . and sorry Alan didn't turn up. And I'm sorry, mate, that you have to spend tomorrow in your boring fucking faceless gargantuan house. But thank fuck I won't be infecting your environment. And thank fuck you had no time or pretended to have no time today you fucking coward or we would have had to have another boring boring boring boring fucking conversation. Dull dull dull like every fucking conversation I have ever had with you. For years. Years. Fucking years . . .

A moment. And then a small contained voice from the phone.

Balfour (*voice-over*) Lorenz. I'm still on the line, Lorenz.

Larry nods, flinches, he is beyond embarrassment and simply hangs up. He blinks and looks at a photo on his phone of him and Richard together . . . laughing, much younger . . . a haiku.

Larry
>hearing footsteps
>and splitting into two –
>a shadow

Larry thinks of his dear brother and folds in on himself.

SCENE FIVE

Reality.
Larry walks into his mother's room. He has two carrier bags and puts them down, plus a huge orange box of washing powder.
Athena watches the television.

Larry Athena. How are you? Richard's very upset . . .

Athena Richard's always upset. I'd have thought it's you who's raging not Richard.

Larry I couldn't find Brasso. But everything else is here. What did you say to him?

Athena You don't want to talk about being cancelled? That's alright. You'll be okay.

Athena indicates for him to empty the two bags, which he does while they speak.

That's a very large box of washing powder. What made you buy that?

Larry It's just . . . practical?

Athena For your house maybe. Impractical for my kitchen. It's gargantuan, and that colour . . . It's very bright. That film last night . . . but Richard got me home which was encouraging that he can still do these things . . . You must have been . . . busy . . . It's all a disaster is it?

Larry It's not great.

Athena No matter, you'll always work . . . And how is the marriage?

Larry Gone.

Athena . . . Good . . .
   You're free. And perhaps you'll be happier now. Freedom is everything, Richard. Your knees will get better, I guarantee.

Larry Larry.

Athena You know why I do that . . . Larry. Lorenz. That box, Larry, can you take it with you? It makes me think of Donald Trump. Theresa is not our tribe, Larry. She spent two thousand pounds on a fridge. With its own camera. So she could see its contents while she was in a supermarket. The woman is insane.

Larry I should never have mentioned that fucking fridge.

Athena I'm glad you did. She said it saved wastage . . . that it was a bargain, in the sale . . . It stopped my ever feeling awkward about asking you for money again.

Larry Mother . . .

Athena You're calling me that more lately. You always called me by my name. Which I liked.

Larry Athena . . . What did you say to Richard?

Athena Have a drink first? There's no hurry . . . Do you think Theresa planned that interview? So she could divorce you? It's her house. Perhaps he'll move in with her? The man. If it's a man?

Larry There is no lover. Theresa didn't even know I was doing a show last night.

Athena She should know. You're her husband. She should have an interest. I think she does have somebody else.

I really do. Why else would she be so hostile? Not just to you but to me? We're obstacles. To her happiness.

Larry Theresa's complex. She has a lot on.

Athena She does nothing.

Larry She's a mature student.

Athena Exactly. I don't think she is complex. I think she's just been in a sulk. For years. So what's going on with this actress? You knew her before?

Larry Nothing's going on.

Athena It didn't look like nothing.

Larry What's this theory? About me and Richard?

Athena I realised something. About you boys . . . But really Larry why else would Theresa dislike me? So intensely? . . . She looks at me as though she wants me dead.

Larry You're always talking to her about breastfeeding. And she couldn't have children.

Athena It might be you not her. You refuse the test . . . How will you live if they don't have you back? You must have a stash. Theresa won't share a thing.

Larry What's this 'idea' about me and Richard?

Athena Alright . . . Now don't get angry. Or feel hurt.

Larry breathes . . . prepares himself.

It's not that I think you're overly strong but what strength you possess . . . I've realised you . . . imbibed it . . . from Richard. In the womb . . . there's always a dominant twin even at embryonic and foetal stage . . . you took his oxygen . . . What?

Larry I'm just . . . listening.

Athena waits . . . Larry breathes . . .

Athena And what do you think?

Larry About depriving my twin of oxygen when I was . . . what, four weeks old?

Athena More like twelve weeks old . . . More developed.

Larry So for the first . . . three months . . . I was innocent of murder . . . I wasn't contemplating fratricide?

Athena I'm not talking about killing . . . just depriving . . . I knew you'd be like this. Some people like a diagnosis. If a doctor says you have 'ADHD' it can be a profound relief. You have a road map.

Larry In this case it would be more Richard's road map of relief wouldn't it? I don't think this gives me any sort of 'map' . . . it just indicates I was an embryonic murderous sociopath.

Athena Here's the thing though and this includes Richard so perhaps you'll be less hostile . . . I'm convinced that there were three of you. And the third child was a girl. And the two of you just eliminated her, in the womb. You bulldozed her into non-existence. I saw a foetus who had died like that. In a museum. She was paper thin. Flat.

Larry Did a doctor ever say that we were originally triplets? Did they?

Athena It's a theory. I didn't say it was fact. But a name came to me . . . Lana.

Larry Lana.

Athena Yes. If you had this sister she should have a name and so she is Lana.

Larry So me and Richard . . . killed? . . . Lana. And then I deprived my twin of oxygen.

Athena I'm not saying it was conscious. You are so spiky, Larry. Just why else is Richard the way he is?

Larry Richard's perfect . . . He finds people . . . challenging. And now he has to fight with this chronic immunity thing . . .

Athena It's his own fault. He went swimming every day. In all weathers.

Larry Cold water's good for you. It was the pollution. It wasn't his fault that the river was chemically polluted.

Athena Fine. But that's the last two years. He's been lost since he was seven years old.

Larry Richard has innate wisdom. He's . . . sensitive . . . if he has to have a label.

Athena He's never had a real job. He's never had a girlfriend.

Larry Manual labour. Gardening. Window cleaning.

Athena He's never had a career . . . He was on meds before this illness. He's a virgin. And he drives you mad with his incessant phone calls . . .

Larry He doesn't . . . it's just . . .

Athena You told me he does.

Larry When I'm stressed . . . when I'm not stressed I enjoy my calls with Richard.

Athena But you're permanently stressed. Richard talked about architecture but he did nothing. Nothing. No real income, no career.

Larry You didn't have a career. You never had any cash.

Athena I was an educator.

Larry laughs despite his anger.

What? What? I know . . . it's an awful American word . . .

Athena laughs now, really laughs. They laugh together.

I didn't ever have any cash because I was a single mother, Larry. I couldn't work could I? Not with you boys. I was a terrible mother. Young . . . alcoholic . . . black-footed hippie. And beautiful. Wasn't I? Beautiful?

She waits for Larry to confirm. He doesn't.

But I was never a bore. Should we get Richard a prostitute?

Larry Stop it. Stop talking about Richard like this.

Athena Like what? . . . Do you think it's inevitable that all children hate their mother?

Larry I don't think it's a given.

Athena Love hate. The phrase sounds so right doesn't it? Rather beautiful. the words entwine . . . You remember when I was sectioned? Terrible word. I always see the brain being knived or strung up or something . . . oh God that film . . . But when I was in there . . . sectioned . . . I ached for you boys. And Richard didn't visit.

Larry He was terrified of the place. He had some idea they would keep him in there. He did try.

Athena And when you visited you'd bring me that awful Lucozade.

Larry Once. I brought it once.

Athena I asked you to make me tea, you were too scared to use their kitchen. You always talked to the other inmates more than you talked to me.

Larry You didn't want to talk. You were silent a lot of the time. I chatted to the others so that they would look out for you.

Athena I was quiet because it was pretty brutal. My back hurt. My spine was damaged with the shock treatment.

Larry I know. And I'm sorry you went through that.

Athena It doesn't matter. Life. Death. What about this prostitute?

Larry Sex worker.

Athena Sorry. Cancel me.

Larry I don't think Richard wants paid sex.

Athena Dear Richard. God the amount of sex you've had. You used to walk around the place so pleased with yourself. It was a sort of . . . fuel. And Richard would just eat his boiled eggs and smile. Richard's an impossible romantic. He wants to find Tess of the d'Urbevilles waiting for him behind his shed but that doesn't happen. Hopeless romantics don't get fucked. What? You look tired.

Larry It's just been . . . a shock.

Athena My theory?

Larry My job . . . losing my home . . .

Athena You're middle-aged but you're mobile. Drink some of that olive oil . . . You've lost a wife but she was a bore. And that house . . . No smoking, no drinking.

Larry Most homes are non-smoking. And her father was an alcoholic.

Athena So was yours . . . You survived. You thrived. You could live here . . . with me. We could divide the flat with a rope.

Larry I'll find somewhere.

Athena I won't drink before three I promise. I won't wake you up unless there's a fire.

Larry I'll rent somewhere. But first I'll go away for a while. Have a bit of quiet.

Athena It doesn't exist, Larry. Quiet. Do you remember the only holiday we went on? I saved all my money . . . to take you boys away. I imagined willow cabins and hibiscus . . . and everything was concrete. And you became hysterical by the pool because I'd gone to the toilet. 'I've lost my mammy!' you shouted. And you put on an Irish accent because all the kids there were from Ireland. That Dublin woman swore you were Irish.

Larry You'd gone to the bar with a man. And left me and Richard by the pool.

Athena I went . . . to buy a drink . . .

Larry You left us in the sunshine and came back when it was night.

Athena You were seven. Quite capable. And you had each other. I would never have left you if you were alone. Richard never reproaches me like you do. He doesn't bleat. Richard has his problems I know but he's more our tribe than you are in many ways . . . You're more . . . conventional . . . I've upset you? Ignore me, Richard . . .

Larry Larry.

Athena I've been fucking vicious in the past but I was deeply unhappy. Now I handle my profound depression with humour and grace. Some children would be proud of me. Wouldn't they?

Larry sighs . . . he can't quite talk.

Larry . . . My first born. You're my lion. I don't care about your deficits. I don't care if sometimes . . . when it mattered most . . . you've been far too scared . . . You were my world in your pre-school years. Then we . . . severed . . . unspoken . . . as mother and child must . . . I let you find your self . . . I made sacrifices, I did . . . my freedom . . . everything . . . I made you boys matching outfits. Didn't I? A mother's love is like no other love. You don't understand . . . But listen . . . here's the thing . . . I've bought a book.

Larry sighs . . . spent.

Larry Yes? I need to go soon.

Athena You're not interested. But it's an important book.

Larry I just don't feel that great right now.

Athena It's non-fiction and it's important, Larry.

Larry Can we talk about it another time? I can just feel my head exploding a bit.

Athena Go then. But it's very rare that I say something is important to me. So I would have appreciated you giving me some time and your attention. But no matter.

Larry (*impatient*) Tell me then! Fucking tell me! . . . Sorry.

Athena You're not. Go away. I don't want anything from you. Just quiet. Go away, Larry.

Larry I can stay here . . . and listen. Sorry.

Athena No I'd rather you fuck off. Fuck off right back to your showbiz worries. And take that box would you?

Larry I haven't really . . . got a home to put it in.

Athena Give it to someone. Or keep it in the car.

Larry I haven't got a car.

Athena Just take it. I can't think of that orange man every time I'm in my kitchen . . . it's just too distracting. It's very Americana.

Larry *Celebrity Shagz.* That's what you call my programme.

Athena It's shorthand. I mean I know you think I've never really achieved very much. But at the same time I'm not cheap. You think my depression is a pain in the arse. And it is. But it's real. As is my pain.

Larry It's been a challenging time.

Athena Don't give it any spin, Larry. Just fuck off and make sure the door locks behind you.

Larry Do you need anything?

Athena I think I just expressed my needs. Pretty clearly.

Larry Sorry I was impatient.

Athena I'm sorry you were impatient too. You'll regret it.

Larry Okay. Goodbye.

Athena Yes . . .

Larry leaves, severely frustrated and depressed. Athena pours herself another drink.

SCENE SIX

Reality.
A restaurant. Larry and Marianne have eaten dinner. Larry drinks wine. Marianne feels impatient with Larry.

Marianne You're not here.

Larry I am . . . sorry . . .

Marianne What was I telling you about?

Larry The mountains near you.

Marianne And what did I do there?

Larry You walked. And . . . and? Sorry . . . you did something else . . .

Marianne It doesn't matter.

Larry tries to reset himself. Everything is more difficult than he had anticipated.

Larry When do you fly back?

Marianne Maybe tomorrow. Or the day after.

Larry Thanks. For meeting. And sorry if I'm . . . distracted . . . I just saw my mother and . . .

Marianne Is she still a bully?

Larry Perhaps we allow ourselves to be bullied. She always said, 'Don't bleat, Larry.' Maybe she was right. I had legs and arms. I have this clicking in my ear and I can't seem to concentrate for very long . . . a few minutes and I'm blasted . . . sorry.

Marianne Maybe you should try speed dating.

Larry Or maybe not.

Marianne starts to feel exhausted by Larry's tension.

Marianne I think I'll go.

Larry Please don't. Athena was only sixteen when she had me and Richard.

Marianne She's not sixteen now is she?

Larry Perhaps her . . . unconventional parenting . . . made me . . . stronger.

Marianne Fuck that. Kids don't need strength. They need love. You needed love. Unconditional love.

And your brother? How is he? The last time I saw him he knelt in front of me and called me his queen.

Larry Richard's in quite a bad way. He has a physical allergy to people and chemicals and mould. He had long Covid. Then he swam every day in his local river and the pollution crashed his immune system which was already weak. It's all very real, he gets sick a lot . . . but no one will recognise it or treat it. So he has to heal himself. His life has got much smaller. He can't work or . . . be . . . in many ways.

Marianne You still pay his way?

Larry This job was useful . . . It could cover Richard and my mother.

Marianne I still don't understand why they suspended you. The ratings were huge . . . it went viral.

Larry . . . Did you really feel our being together was . . . wrong in New York?

Marianne It wasn't something I'd ever voiced to myself before . . . the age thing . . . but you weren't listening . . . and I suddenly felt angry and I thought yeah why didn't you just leave me be . . .

Larry And you didn't think it might be damaging? To say those things? On TV?

Marianne Fuck damage. Maybe you damaged me. Maybe there was nothing illegal going on but I was a kid and you were reckless.

Larry We were all permanently pissed, Marianne.

Marianne So . . . it wasn't what? Real?

Larry It was more than real. You blew me away with your honesty and your beauty. And we laughed, Marianne. Didn't we . . . I was completely in love with you.

Marianne Not completely . . . You fucked someone else while we were together.

Larry It was one night. You'd gone away. I can't even remember her face. Or name.

Marianne I was away for three weeks . . . it's not so very long . . . I couldn't comprehend how you could be next to someone else's skin and smell . . . when we were . . . us. And then the lies.

Larry Because it meant nothing. And I knew with what had happened to you . . . it would make you spiral down . . . But it was like you sensed it. You were ill with it. Your face changed . . . everything about you was worn out and you weren't eating and I thought I'd made you actually sick . . . So I told you.

Marianne Not before I hit my head against the wall. To make you tell me the truth.

Larry But I did tell you. And I apologised and apologised.

Marianne And then you just . . . left.

Larry I'd fucked it up. I imagined you couldn't forgive me.

Marianne And you could just leave like that?

Larry I'd shattered us. And you were going to have an amazing career, I could see that.

Marianne So your silence and absence . . . it was a sacrifice? A noble act?

Larry I was sorry. And I am still . . . sorry.

Marianne But not to say . . . anything. Just to . . . leave a gap. I rang and rang.

Larry I was . . . ashamed . . . I genuinely felt you had this huge life to live and yes I was older and . . .

Marianne You knew my history. You knew how fragile I was.

Larry And I fucked up. Once. On a single very drunken night.

Marianne It doesn't matter.

Larry . . . I'd like your . . . forgiveness . . . your blessing.

Marianne is quiet . . . withdrawn.

Marianne Fuck you, Larry . . . I couldn't . . . function. For a while. When you left.

Larry But you've thrived . . .

Marianne It's a strange word.

Larry You've done brilliant beautiful work.

Marianne You sound like a teacher . . .

Larry shrugs, he doesn't know what to say.

Larry Can I come back with you? . . . to your hotel. Tonight.

Marianne laughs.

Marianne Because you've been chucked out.

Larry Because I love you.

Marianne And your wife?

Larry We're over. We're done. And that was before all of this.

Marianne Do you know why? What made you fall out of love?

Larry I don't know if we were ever in love. Just . . . we seemed to help each other. We fitted well. And then we didn't.

Marianne What made you misfit?

Larry We have a fridge. Theresa really wanted it. It has its own camera. You can talk to it.

Marianne Fuck. She talks to the fridge.

Larry I don't think they have conversations. But she can say 'cheese' and it shows an image. Of cheese in one of its drawers. Something like that.

Marianne Right.

Larry And at night in the kitchen I would stare at it . . . and its humming sounded very loud to me . . . and its blue light when I opened it . . . made me disproportionately sad . . .

I kept thinking of that white enamel bucket we had on the fire escape? You filled it with water and kept the milk in it. I would keep my hand in the cold water a few seconds before grabbing the milk. And then I would think of the dog I used to feed when it bounded up those metal steps . . .

Marianne You shouldn't have fed that dog. It confused him. And you took it to the vet. That was crazy.

Larry To try and heal an animal?

Marianne . . . Let nature take its course.

Larry Would you feel the same way about humans?

Marianne If I came into the hospital and you had tubes and you couldn't be yourself I'd rip them out.

Larry breathes . . . looks at Marianne and takes her hand.

Marianne What?

Larry I would watch you when you were asleep. And I thought dying wouldn't be so bad as long as you were next to me.

Marianne I watched you asleep too. I liked you sleeping. Quiet. But all this . . . nostalgia . . . it's not useful.

Larry *Nostos* . . . return. And home. *Algos* . . . pain.

Marianne We're not each other's home. The damage I had before you . . . I never got rid of it.

Larry Why would you? Is he still alive? I wanted to kill him that time I met him with your mother.

Marianne You punched him. I felt euphoric.

Larry It's the only time I've ever hit anyone.

Marianne No one had ever done that for me. You did it so beautifully. He fell on the floor and covered his face. 'Not my head,' he said. I was so proud . . . I did a lot of drugs in LA . . . got a bit you know . . . hooked . . . Now I just take . . . meds. So . . . relationships are kind of out.

Larry What are you doing tomorrow? Do you want to come and meet my mother?

Marianne That's a definite no.

Larry I met yours . . .

Marianne I am . . . pretty fucking busy, Larry, I have to meet this guy who wants to make a documentary about the history of refugee camps . . . I said I'd narrate the film for him . . . He's quite intense.

Larry A director?

Marianne And he's producing it. We're going to have a chat.

Larry I sort of forgot for a moment that you have a life . . . a job . . .

Marianne Because you don't?

Marianne's not being cruel, just trying to break some tension. They might even laugh.

Larry You could stay.

Marianne You're talking to me like I'm nineteen.

Larry . . . So where are you going to meet this fervent director?

Marianne I didn't say he was fervent. I've never met him.

Larry Does he say 'Copy that'?

Marianne My friend says that. He's wonderful.

Larry This director's lazy. He's relying on a mesmeric actress to make his film less boring.

Marianne Actor, Larry. I'm an actor. You're very behind the times.

Larry Fervent meant hot originally . . . or glowing . . . I don't imagine he's any of that.

Marianne You're jealous? Of someone who doesn't exist yet? Meeting your mother . . . It's involvement . . . It's like meeting your kid or something. Athena was always more like your child than your mother.

Larry You might love her. People do.

Marianne I won't. She's been cruel to you. And I don't want to be your fucking girlfriend. And I don't want us to spend tonight together. And I don't really even want to be here.

Larry I'll order you a cab?

Marianne I'll order myself a cab! I'm not a child! . . . I'm going to smoke now. Order me a double espresso and choose a pudding for me? I just remembered Athena's real name.

Larry Marianne.

Marianne Yeah?

Larry Nothing.

Marianne What?

Larry It doesn't matter.

Marianne It does. Everything matters. Everything we say right now is pretty important.

Larry . . . Your hands . . . and your arms . . . the shapes that they make . . . that hasn't changed really . . .

Marianne What about my face?

Larry It's wonderful to see your face too . . . and everything . . .

Marianne Be quiet . . . I'm great. I'm a movie star. And you sell suitcases. And you're homeless. And you're hot.

Marianne loves Larry and kisses him.
    She walks outside.

Larry sits alone, spent, raw . . .

Larry
A bat swoops past –
The wife from across the street
Glances my way

Larry pours a glass of wine and downs it in one.

He hums 'There's a Small Hotel' and plays the rhythm of it on the table.
    Sequinned light happens and Larry stands, gently taps and shuffles a routine with his feet . . . hopeful and fearful . . . deeply felt and enamoured.

Larry sings the third and fourth verses of the song.

SCENE SEVEN

Reality.
    A hotel room. Darkness.
    Marianne and Larry walk through the door. Larry is a bit drunk.

Marianne I have to put the card in.

Larry Or not . . . We could just stay in the dark.

Marianne puts the key card in. The light is bright. She tries several switches and they are all different levels of light and brightness. Larry looks at a hanger with a long flowing negligee on it.

Do you wear this? Bloody hell . . .

Marianne They sent it to me. From my last film.

Larry You're a rock star, Marianne. I've seen so many pictures of you over the years. The parties. The premieres.

Marianne I'd rather look at plants growing out of the cracks of a stone wall than be at a party. But . . . I get invited. And you?

Larry Not so much now. And when I do go I always attract the bore and I can't get away.

Marianne You look them straight in the eye . . . you put your hand here on their arm, and you say, 'It's been really nice talking to you.' And then you go. And they're happy. They've been 'seen'.

Larry It probably works better if you're a movie star.

Marianne Try it. Now.

Larry I'll try it at the bus stop. I'll probably be spending a lot of time at bus stops.

Marianne I'll do it to you if you ever get boring. Will you ever get boring, Larry?

Larry I'm often boring. But not with you.

Larry shrugs.

Marianne Because we're honest. We have history.

Larry Epic . . . history . . .

Marianne I did miss you. Shit . . . You wouldn't leave my head. I had this rush of . . . when I saw you selling those suitcases.

Larry Briefcases.

Marianne If I came into your shop would you sell me one?

Larry I would. Absolutely. And you would have no regret.

Marianne No regret.

Larry Because it's not just any briefcase. It's an executive briefcase. It's durable. It has a TSA lock . . . and it's . . . If I tell you . . .

Marianne Tell me.

Larry It's water-resistant . . . So . . . Are you going to buy it? Or are you a timewaster?

Marianne I'll buy it.

Larry Good. I don't like timewasters.

Marianne I do like wasting time though.

Larry You mustn't do that. It's . . .

Larry shrugs. Loves Marianne. He kisses her.

Larry Tell me how you waste your time, Marianne. Tell me what you do.

Marianne I mooch. I walk a lot . . . and sometimes if I'm feeling really disconnected . . .

Larry Yes.

Marianne I go to the mountains and I dig my own grave in the woods . . . I lie down when I'm done . . . It's shallow . . . and I'm sweating and tired and my hands are burning from the digging and the earth is freezing and I lie there for a while . . . looking up at the stars . . . and when the cold starts to hurt I get up. It's like . . . a rehearsal. And I've given up love . . . I mean occasionally I . . . find someone . . . and we . . . embrace.

Larry Don't tell me that part.

Marianne You asked.

Larry But you can't have given up love?

Marianne puts the negligee on over her clothes. She holds his arm gently and incants . . .

Marianne It's been really nice talking to you.

Indicates for him jokily to go away.

Larry I refuse though. To go away.

Marianne But it's been Really Nice talking to you.

Marianne laughs and indicates for him to go away.

Now fuck off . . . man in trousers.

Larry No I'm staying. I'm going to bore you to death, Marianne Barre . . . And I will hold your hand in death. And I will lie in that shallow grave with you in the woods and I'll look up to the stars with you . . . and perhaps you won't even be dead and we'll just lie down beside each other . . . breathing . . .

Marianne But the earth is very cold.

Larry We'll get up. We'll climb a tree. We won't be dead. We'll be alive. We'll refuse. To leave.

They breathe together, looking at one another. Larry touches her arm.

It's been really nice talking to you.

Marianne nods, she doesn't want to go away either.

It's been Really Nice . . .
  It's been really nice talking to you . . . now go away . . .

Marianne half nods . . . breathes . . . bursts into tears.

Marianne . . . Marianne . . . it was . . . we were playing . . .

But Marianne is inconsolable . . . she buries her head in her hands.

Please . . . my love . . . please . . .

And Larry kisses her face and Marianne turns away from him but he holds her and finally she turns back and kisses him too.

The Waitress from the café stands in the shadows at a microphone and sings the third verse of 'There's a Small Hotel' in a thirties style . . .

Larry and Marianne dance closely together, gentle, felt.

Larry undresses and Marianne puts the negligee on him. They dance gently until they stop in the shadows. Silence as they look at each other for some moments. Breathing.

Marianne touches Larry's face.
Kisses his neck.

Marianne You sleep. Close your eyes.

Marianne sings and hums 'The Leaving of Liverpool' as Larry leans into her. He is exhausted . . .

So fare-thee-well, my own true love
When I return, united we will be
It's not the leaving of Liverpool that grieves me
But my darling, when I think of thee . . .

Marianne stands Larry up and takes a few steps away from him.

I was ten weeks pregnant when you left me in New York. I didn't know until a week after you'd gone . . . I had an abortion. I had to walk past these two women who were crying and shouting outside the clinic. Shaking their banners. They were more upset than I was. They gave me a leaflet with these pretty intense pictures and I went in . . .

Larry You didn't tell me. All those messages but you didn't say.

Marianne You didn't return my calls . . . It was my body. My affair. I had no doubts. Nor would you have. It was simply a problem. A bit painful. And I was sad. It was very . . . difficult. But telling you . . . how would that have helped or changed anything? . . . Funny that neither of us had kids. I'm going to leave now. I need a cigarette.

Larry I would have come back. Just to . . .

Marianne I think you would. But it's better to do these things alone sometimes.

Marianne leaves and Larry follows her.

SCENE EIGHT

Reality.
Athena drinks wine, Marianne and Larry drink tea in Athena's house.

Athena You sure you don't want a proper drink, Marianne? You don't mind that I do? You enjoyed yourself on the television the other night . . .

Marianne It was . . . good to see Larry.

Athena You played it very well.

Marianne I wasn't playing . . .

Athena Isn't that your job though? With the audience. I was blessed with never having a steady job. Have you met Richard yet?

Marianne I met him. When I was here before.

Athena I heard so much about yours and Larry's first wave. Richard's wonderful. He inherited all the poetry from me. He's more Irish than Larry . . . the Irish love ghosts . . . When was Marianne here, Larry?

Larry In 2000. We celebrated the millennium together.

Athena But you hid her from me?

Marianne . . . You were in hospital.

Athena Ah . . .

Larry You were in the Maudsley.

Athena Well yes . . . that was my second home wasn't it? I can tell you which psychiatric wards are best Marianne if ever you need them . . . Which one has the nicest smoking garden. Or rooftop. Richard lived with me during that time he was wonderful around the house. Soup. Hoover. All of that. I was very much alone in the wards though. Larry was in New York.

Larry For two years. I was away for two years. I was here the rest of the time.

Athena I'm reading a wonderful book, Marianne. I thought it would be impossible to buy . . . or it would be on the dark web . . . but it turns out it's a *New York Times* bestseller . . . it's a fucking bestseller, Richard. I can't really reach a way out of my depression . . . So the decision is pretty simple. I'm going to end my life. And this book is an aid to that. It shows you various ways. Painless . . . And you can do it alone so you boys don't have to aid and abet.

Larry What? What are you saying?

Athena Suicide. I've been thinking about it for years. My foot is worse. And they said it might need cutting off and I just can't go there.

Larry Your foot is the smoking . . . they told you to stop smoking . . .

Athena I can't be in a hospital. And Larry refuses to live with me.

Marianne Larry . . . I'll leave you two to talk.

Athena Don't go. You need to stay.

Larry I'd live with you if that changed your mind.

Athena Would you? Really?

Larry thinks for a moment. Athena takes this as a rejection.

Dr Shah has given me a huge prescription of morphine for the next month. To kill the pain. He's fantastic. If the book is not useful . . . I'll take all of it.

Larry He could be prosecuted.

Athena He's done nothing wrong.

Larry You're talking about it so casually.

Marianne I really should go, Athena.

Athena No! He'll blame me if you go. Listen to me. We might need you. Your opinion. Stay!

Larry Leave if you want to, Marianne. I'll meet you at the train station.

Athena Larry. I want to die while I can still remember everything. And I'm in almost constant pain.

Larry You can't do it. I'll . . . call the police.

Athena laughs.

Athena Come here.

Larry goes to her. Athena enfolds him.

My Larry. My lion. If you could see the depression. It's a desert. And you know how much I loved water. I'll never swim again. Or run again. Or make love again . . . The life . . . the joy . . . it's gone. You're both grown you and Richard . . . And I want to check out of this crazy hotel. Which is by the way absolutely on fire anyway . . . I may be exiting just moments before the world explodes . . . I would go away and do it but all that fucking traveling and no holiday at the end of it. I want to do it here on principle. I'll do it when you're away sometime . . . I'll arrange things with the police and leave notes . . . so you don't have to find me . . . and then just leave me at the morgue. No funeral. Just you two and Richard have a night of it. And you, Marianne. Raise a glass to me.

Larry . . . We need to get someone professional involved. To help you change your mind.

Athena My mind is the one thing I have left. Don't mangle me. Please . . . It's been an idea for years . . .

Larry A joke, Mother. Not a serious idea.

Athena Now seems timely.

Larry You mean it . . .

Athena I do.

Larry No.

Athena There's nothing left for me. Do you see?

And they sit together, silent for some moments. Larry tries to understand.

Marianne? Thank you for staying. Would you like some marijuana? I have some little roll-ups here? With just a spider's leg of weed in them . . .

Marianne I do have to go. I'm catching a train.

Athena It will make the station and the journey far more pleasant. Where are you going?

Marianne I'm going to the North.

Athena From Euston? I like the North. You'll make Richard very happy.

Larry Larry, Mother. And can we just . . .

Athena Or Richard? Marianne is free to choose. You were an alcoholic weren't you?

Larry sighs.

Marianne We all drank a lot.

Athena Yes that's alcoholism. How are your knees, Larry? They bug him. And you were an addict?

Larry Mother . . .

Marianne . . . Not so much now.

Athena I speak of these things without shame attached, Marianne. What will you do with my son?

Marianne I . . . don't have a plan.

Athena laughs.

Are you falling back in love with Larry?

Marianne Yes.

Athena Good. Richard is a virgin and hermetic and Larry is wonderful. But he's prone to being rather cheap.

Marianne Larry's not cheap.

Larry starts to slap his ear.

Athena What is it, Larry? What's wrong?

Larry There's something . . . I keep hearing something . . .

Athena A cockroach.

Larry I did ask you not to drink.

Athena Don't you think . . . interviewing . . . making a living just being . . . intrusive . . . it's shabby . . . Acting though? It must be interesting, pretending to be other people?

Marianne It's more like . . . a communion. And I believe it's needed. We're in dark times.

Athena Show me a time that wasn't dark, Marianne?

Athena is starting to feel the darkness of drink. A switch is clicking.

You're quite hostile.

Marianne I really should go now.

Athena If you get ill or anything terrifying happens Larry will walk out . . . You keep doing your work though. While you can. Knock 'em dead.

Larry Let's go.

Athena You can't take the truth, Larry. Richard can. He's stronger than you. Larry simply . . . hovers . . . or you glide . . . or navigate. You don't actually feel things, that's your trouble.

Larry We've covered this territory before haven't we? Many times.

Marianne Perhaps Larry found it hard to feel? Perhaps he was scared to?

Athena He was. Always. It's not an attractive trait. Being terrified.

Marianne But he has survived. I'm sorry you're in pain.

Athena I was pregnant with my boys and my father put me on the back of his bicycle . . . in the middle of the night . . . and he cycled me five miles in the dark and the rain to the Mothers' Home and he left me there . . . but I ran away . . . I kept my boys . . . I never saw my sister again. A few telephone calls. Then nothing.

Marianne sees that the damage is not reparable.

Marianne You were brave . . . to leave.

Athena I missed my sister like someone had torn a leg off.

Athena becomes removed: part reverie, part mourning. They wait for her.

Well I think she's wonderful, Larry. You must marry her. She's the one and perhaps Marianne you can help him to be less . . . ?

Marianne Goodbye Athena.

Larry I'll come with you. Take you to the station.

Marianne Stay.

Athena I need Larry to stay.

Marianne He's staying.

Athena But not to go away too.

Marianne That'll be Larry's decision.

Athena Larry's never made a real decision in his life.

Marianne I love your son. He is brave and he is beautiful. And he makes me laugh. Your real name . . . it's Debbie.

Athena I'm not a Debbie.

Marianne It's a good name. Debbie Reynolds. Debbie Harry . . .

Athena I am Athena. Goddess of Wisdom.

Marianne And I am Marianne. Goddess of Liberty.

Larry I love you Marianne.

Marianne You've always loved me. We've always loved . . . each other . . . Goodbye Larry . . . Athena . . .

Athena I need him, Marianne.

Marianne I see that. Life is so much about timing as well as love isn't it . . . I'll see you soon, Larry.

Marianne leaves. Larry looks at his mother.

Athena She loves your flaws. Presumably you love hers. It's all rather sad.

Larry kisses his mother's forehead and starts to leave.

Larry Goodbye Mother.

Athena I have my morphine. I have enough of it. So yes, goodbye Larry.

Larry Mother . . .

Athena Or simply kill me if you'd prefer me not to take it. I'd prefer that . . . This girl, Larry . . .

Larry Woman.

Athena This girl, she won't be faithful to you . . . you won't be enough for her. How could you be?

Larry I think I could.

Athena She's broken in some way.

Larry So am I.

Athena You're not. You're not broken.

Larry I am myself. With Marianne. Very completely. My self.

Athena That's just . . . the talk of an idiot. She needs someone real. Vibrant. Someone who is truly authentic.

Larry I could very easily kill you, Mother.

Athena Do it. There's that ridiculous Japanese knife that Richard saved up for. Cut me.

Athena and Larry stare at each other. Athena laughs. And now she cries hard.

Larry I'll get you a glass of water. From the kitchen.

Athena I don't need it. I don't need water. Just go . . . do go . . . now . . . and be with her. Just go. My Larry. Off you go. Don't be late.

Larry leaves. Athena is consumed with anger and jealousy. But craves love and beauty too.

See how they love!
If I am reborn, let me be
A butterfly in the field

Athena knows that she will not see her Larry again.

SCENE NINE

Reality.
   Larry walks but feels a huge and painful blow to his stomach. He is blasted with the impact of the pain.

A Dream.
   A sunny place. A slight breeze. Larry recovers and Marianne sits opposite him. A Los Angeles Receptionist passes, elegant, dressed entirely in black.

Receptionist Can I get you anything?

Larry We're good thanks. You look great.

Receptionist Oh thank you! I'm going to a funeral!

The Receptionist laughs and smiles hugely.

Just . . . sit anywhere.

Larry and Marianne sit on the ground.

You had the knee pain?

Larry It's gone. Thank you.

Receptionist The air here is so much cleaner.

Larry Should we have brought things? With us? Do we stay here or are we billeted somewhere else?

Receptionist Just relax. There are no rules you see? Only don't look back . . . Was there anything else you wanted?

Marianne I don't think so.

Receptionist Wonderful.

The Receptionist leaves.

Larry What happened?

Marianne You happened. To me. And I was so glad.

Larry Marianne? Will you kiss me? Take away this rushing in my ear?

Marianne Put on your clothes. This isn't happening.

But Marianne is gone.

SCENE TEN

Reality.
Euston Station.
Larry talks to Richard on the phone. Larry walks quickly and is agitated, he is hurt badly and in shock. There is blood under his jacket.

Larry . . . You need to ring the police . . . my eardrums are about to explode . . .

Richard Where are you? Who's with you? Why do you need the police?

Larry I was trying to find Marianne . . . but there's this huge crowd . . . Maybe it's the Carnival . . . So many people. I've lost her. I was taking out cash . . .

Richard There's no carnival. It's winter. What's happened? Show me your face?

Larry My knees . . . I can't feel them . . . and my eyes . . . My eyes belong to someone else . . .

Richard They're yours . . . show me your eyes . . . Larry? Are you hurt?

Larry This creep was shouting at Marianne and I ran up to him and I pushed him but it wasn't her . . . just from a distance she looked . . . and then I bought a pill off a guy . . .

Richard Why? Larry?

Larry I don't know . . . And then the money . . . I took it out of a hole . . . in the wall . . . I love you Richard . . . take care . . . don't do anything stupid . . . I can't feel my legs . . .

Athena pours some wine and puts a vial of pills into it. She takes out a cigarette and her Zippo lighter. She moves her ashtray and glass from one place to another.

Larry stares at the lights as trains zoom by . . . He lies down, wounded.

   Ava approaches him and sits next to him and waits, on her phone.

Larry is bleeding. Ava is on the phone.

Ava Yeah he's breathing . . . but there's a lot of blood . . . Someone stabbed him . . . at a cashpoint. You need to come soon yeah?

Ava folds her scarf and opens Larry's shirt and presses the cloth against Larry's wound . . . She wears a name badge.

Unless you're a doctor can you not stand around staring?

Larry Ava . . .

Ava Yeah . . . You're going to be okay.

Larry Ava . . .

Ava What's your name?

Larry Larry . . .

Ava Larry. Just breathe.

Larry I won't make this evening. I'm not at my best.

Ava Just concentrate on breathing. In and out that's all. They're going to patch you up in a bit.

Larry And we're in Liverpool. And the speed dating? Your eye is better. Your eye . . .

Ava I work in the opticians over there. I saw a guy come up to you at the machine.

Larry It was blunt. Like a cricket bat.

Ava Maybe . . . don't talk too much . . .

Larry I thought I was in a forest. That my brother had hit me with a branch. We climbed trees. A lot. And sat in them and talked . . . Who hit me?

Ava A boy . . . stabbed you. He was young . . . maybe seventeen.

Larry My ears . . . It's like the sea . . . the clicking's gone.

Ava Shall I call someone on your phone?

Larry Richard can't do stations . . . Don't worry them. Nor my. Mother . . . Tell Marianne . . . tell her I'm checking out of this crazy hotel.

Ava Is she in your phone?

Larry She's everywhere. It's just . . . emptying. I might close my eyes for a bit.

Ava You have to stay awake. Okay? Don't close your eyes.

Athena approaches. And holds Larry. Ava leaves.

Athena I've got you, Larry . . . I remember seeing you first . . . you wouldn't open your eyes for a week and I kept wondering when you would . . . and when you did . . . your eyes, Larry . . . and you always wanted so much it was beautiful how much you wanted. You come with me now . . . I've got you . . . I love you. To the moon and back, my Larry . . . All the tea in China . . .

Larry I want to see Marianne? Can I?

Marianne appears and sits down next to Larry.

Marianne Larry I was in this place . . . an old children's home . . . empty bunk beds . . . and there was a window . . . and I climbed up and stared out of it . . . and I broke the mesh glass with an iron bar . . . and there was sky . . . wisps of white cloud . . . and no one could tell me what to do . . . and I love you Larry . . . I love your courage and your smell and the shape of your legs . . . and your skin's patterns . . . and that will be good for you there . . . knowing that you're beloved . . . I need a coffee some caffeine . . . how long will you live for? . . . I wish we could play tennis together. I don't play . . . I'm too scruffy . . . all those white clothes . . . the ocean is so loud . . . I can hear it in your blood . . . and I am you Larry . . . I am you.

And Marianne kisses him and leaves.

Athena Just let go now. Everything is there.

Larry What if it isn't?

Athena There's white noise. A lot of humming. It's not a departure, Larry, it's a return.

Larry dies in Athena's arms.

Marianne stands at the microphone and sings for him, bereft, the third and fourth verses of 'There's a Small Hotel'.

Marianne stops singing abruptly and stares at the audience.

She starts to dance . . . just dancing her grief and pain. Lines of top-hatted dancing men are projected and she dances against them . . . until she sits down, spent.

Richard laughs. He writes on his hand.

Blackout.

SCENE ELEVEN

Reality.
Marianne lies in a shallow grave. Richard lies in a shallow grave a couple of feet away from her.

We see them vertically as though they are standing, as though we are watching them from above.

Marianne What else?

Richard In school? One boy . . . very handsome . . . he teased me badly. And his sister called Larry Lorenzo which he hated. So Larry went up to him . . . Larry's in his viscose trousers . . . always covered in mud . . . and he just pisses on this boy. In front of everyone.

Marianne I'm glad. Did the boy beat him up?

Richard Absolutely. Him and his gang beat us both up. Blood . . . mud . . . We walked home in fits of laughter. Larry kept laughing about the pissing bit. We were in bits.

Marianne And what did your mother say?

Richard She laughed too. And she gave me a cigarette to take away my toothache.

Marianne How old were you?

Richard Twelve? . . . Good times.

Marianne And?

Richard And we loved that walk to school. The hedgerow. The foxes in the morning. Seeing our own breath in the cold. Pissing and watching the steam.

Marianne And did the boy stop bullying you?

Richard No but I was no longer scared of him. And we'd, you know . . . we had roared and that was enough.

Marianne stares at the sky.

Marianne No stars.

Richard No, but the beauty of those inky clouds . . . and the sky is better from down here.

Marianne . . . I hate to think of his hands being cold . . . You tell a good story, Richard.

Richard Larry is the storyteller. You can call me Larry if you like. Mother always did. She couldn't do names after her treatment, names became dislocated . . . You know trees talk to each other . . . they communicate. It's a fact. They protect each other. Like siblings. If a tree has blight it sends messages . . . through its roots and the neighbouring tree it receives the SOS and it retracts its own roots . . . I am sorry. I'm so sorry.

Marianne We all crash around . . . and . . .

Richard We do.

Marianne stares at the sky. Richard looks at his hand with a torch. There is writing on it.

Marianne What does it say?

Richard My memory is shot . . . and all of this will just . . .

He breathes hard. He shows it to her.

Can you decipher it? I have terrible writing. So does Larry. The last word is . . .

Marianne nods.

Marianne I can read it.

Richard nods.

Richard I might just be quiet now . . . I'm not allowed to touch anyone. I get sick. With this illness. But you're alright?

Marianne I'm fine . . . I am . . . I don't need you to touch me.

They look up at the night clouds, hearts broken . . .
   Marianne breathes hard . . . tries not to cry.
   She grips at the earth beneath her with her hands, bereft.
   Richard reaches out.
   And he takes her hand.
   And they lie together, quiet, side by side.

The End.